WHAT IT MEANS TO BE
SERIES

PUBLISHER	Joseph R. DeVarennes
PUBLICATION DIRECTOR	Kenneth H. Pearson
ADVISORS	Roger Aubin
	Robert Furlonger
EDITORIAL MANAGER	Jocelyn Smyth
EDITORS	Ann Martin
	Shelley McGuinness
	Robin Rivers
	Mayta Tannenbaum
ARTISTS	Summer Morse
	Barbara Pileggi
	Steve Pileggi
	Mike Stearns
PRODUCTION MANAGER	Ernest Homewood
PRODUCTION ASSISTANTS	Catherine Gordon
	Kathy Kishimoto
PUBLICATION ADMINISTRATOR	Anna Good

Canadian Cataloguing in Publication Data

Elliot, Jacqueline
   What it means to be—a family

(What it means to be; 9)
ISBN 0-7172-2230-6

1. Family — Moral and ethical aspects — Juvenile literature.
I. Pileggi, Steve.   II. Title.   III. Title: A family.   IV. Series.

HQ734.E44 1987   j173   C87-095050-9

WHAT IT MEANS TO BE . . .

A FAMILY

Written by
Jacqueline Elliot

Illustrated by
Steve Pileggi

Being part of a family makes you feel good.

Ryan came home from school looking glum. When his father asked him what was wrong he said, "My teacher got angry at me today. She said I was talking too much in the library, but it wasn't me." Then he added sadly, "She didn't even let me explain."

Ryan's father walked over and gave him a big hug. "Don't worry, Ryan, I believe you. I'm sure things will be better tomorrow." Ryan brightened up a little.

"Now how about helping me make dinner?" his father suggested. "We're having your favorite tonight—fried chicken and coleslaw."

"Sure, Dad," answered Ryan, smiling.

Family members make you feel better when things go wrong.

Family members enjoy spending time with each other.

Janice and Jason were eating breakfast one Saturday morning when their father said, "I have a surprise for you."

"What?" asked Janice.

"Tell us, tell us," said Jason excitedly.

"Your mother and I have been working very hard lately and so have you two at school. Today we'll all take the day off and go somewhere special as a treat."

"Where?" the children asked.

"We're going to the zoo," replied their mother.

Janice and Jason wandered around the zoo with their parents. They saw crocodiles sunning themselves, penguins parading around, polar bears splashing in their pool and lots of snakes. They stopped in front of the tigers' cage. They were Janice's favorite animal. She loved hearing them growl and watching them pace back and forth. Jason was a little bit frightened of them.

When they got to the monkeys' cage, Jason crouched and swung his arms up and down. He chattered like a monkey and hopped from one foot to the other. His parents and sister started laughing. He soon joined in. It was fun to be at the zoo together.

Being part of a family means sharing activities.

Everyone in a family must share responsibilities.

Bobby was on his way downstairs when the doorbell rang. It was Jason. They were going to the playground.

Just as Bobby was about to leave, his father said, "Bobby, you promised to help me clean out the garage this afternoon."

Bobby had forgotten all about it. He was very disappointed. "Sorry, Jason," he murmured. "You'd better go ahead. I'll come along later if I can."

"Okay, see you later," Jason said.

As Bobby and his father tidied and swept the garage, they kept stumbling upon all sorts of treasures.

"Look," said Bobby's father, "this is the cradle you slept in when you were a baby."

"Did I really fit in there?" asked Bobby, laughing at its size.

"You sure did—but not for very long."

"And here is my first bicycle with training wheels," cried Bobby.

"Remember how excited you were when you got it?" his father asked. They both laughed.

Soon the garage was neat and clean.

Being part of a family means sharing chores and memories.

Being part of a family gives you a sense of belonging.

Joey went outside when he heard his friends' voices. Ryan, Mitchell, Tammy and Janice were standing in front of his house. They were holding brightly colored eggs.

"Where are your eggs?" asked Janice.

"Yes, what did you get for Easter?" said Ryan.

"We don't celebrate Easter," replied Joey.

"Gee, look what you're missing," cried Mitchell, holding up his eggs.

When Joey went back inside, he said, "Mom, all the other kids have Easter eggs and I don't. It makes me feel left out."

"We have different customs than your friends and I know it must be hard sometimes," said his mother quietly. "But you know your father and I love you very much. Maybe as a special treat we'll go to a movie tonight. Would you like that?"

Sometimes friends can make you feel left out. Remember that you are always part of your family.

Being part of a family means being thoughtful when a relative is sick.

When Tammy and Colette's mother hung up the phone the girls knew something was wrong. "I have some bad news. Your grandmother had an accident. She slipped and hurt her leg and is in the hospital."

"Oh, Mom, that's terrible," said Colette. Tammy looked like she was going to cry.

"Now, don't worry. Grandma will be fine. I do want to go see her at the hospital right away though. I'll ask David from down the street to come and look after you until your father gets home."

Once their mother left Tammy and Colette were sad and worried. "Why don't you make something to cheer up your grandmother?" David said.

"That's a great idea!" Colette exclaimed. "We can make her a mobile."

"Sure, and I can help," offered David.

A few days later the girls went to the hospital with their mother.

When they arrived their grandmother beamed at them from the bed. "Here, Grandma," said Tammy as she held up the mobile they had made. "Colette and I made this for you." It was covered with bright flowers.

"I hope you like it," Colette added.

"What a nice surprise! You two are so thoughtful. Since my hip operation I can't move easily and I do get tired of television. I can hang it over my bed."

When someone in your family is unwell, you can use your imagination to think of something to cheer them up.

Sometimes family members have to give up something to help each other.

Tammy and Colette stared out the living room window waiting for their father. He had gone to pick up their grandmother at the hospital. She was coming to stay with them.

"There she is!" cried Tammy.

"How are you feeling?" Colette asked.

"A little bit tired, dear," answered Grandma. "I think I'll have a nap."

Tammy and Colette went to Colette's room to play. Soon they were fighting.

"Don't touch *my* things," Colette yelled.

"But I'm bored," whined Tammy.

"Get out of my room!" shouted Colette.

Their mother appeared. "Girls, your grandmother is trying to sleep," she said quietly. "You know you have to share a room while she's with us, so please try to get along."

"I'm sorry," murmured Colette.

"Me too," said Tammy.

Family members help each other. Remember that everyone must make sacrifices once in a while.

Pets are part of the family.

Joey was racing out the door to play ball in the park. "Bye, Mom. See you later," he said.

"Just a minute Joey," called his mother from the kitchen. "Didn't you forget something?"

Joey ran back in. A small yellow dog wagged his tail and stood by his empty bowl.

"Remember how you promised to look after Muffin when we first got him?" asked his mother.

"Sure Mom, I remember. Don't worry, Muffin," said Joey. "I'll feed you right away. And I'll take you for a walk after I play ball." Muffin licked Joey's hand and wagged his tail even harder.

Part of being a family member is sharing the responsibility for pets.

Sometimes parents get divorced or separated.

Jason and Dylan were walking home from school together. "Do you have all of your projects ready for parents' night?" Jason asked.

"Sure," replied Dylan. "I finished my last drawing on Tuesday."

"Are your parents coming?"

"Well my dad is," said Dylan, "but my mom doesn't live here. Dad and Mom are divorced."

"Oh," mumbled Jason. He felt bad for asking, but Dylan didn't look upset.

At supper Jason said, "Did you know that Dylan's parents are divorced? His mother even lives in another city. I think that's sad."

"Well," said his father, "some marriages don't work out. Often it's better for people to get a divorce than to stay together and be unhappy."

"But Dylan probably never sees his mom. He must miss her," sighed Jason.

"I'm sure he sees her on holidays," said his mother. "It must be hard for him at times, but Dylan looks happy to me."

The next day after school, Jason and Dylan were playing catch. Jason said, "Do you miss your mom? I mean, are you sad that you don't live with her?"

"Sometimes I miss her," Dylan answered thoughtfully, "but most of the time it's okay. I really like going on the train to visit her. And we always have fun when we're together. I also like living with my dad. We get along well. And I know they both love me."

Even if parents are divorced or separated they still love their children.

Families have memories to share.

Hannah and Kim were playing at Tammy and Colette's house.

Colette said, "Did I ever show you the pictures of last year's Hallowe'en party?"

"No," replied Kim, "I didn't see them."

"Me neither," answered Hannah.

Colette went up to her bedroom and pulled out a picture album. When the girls saw the photographs of the Hallowe'en costumes, they giggled.

"Here are pictures of Tammy and me when we were babies," said Colette smiling. "And here is a picture of our old dog," added Tammy.

"I love looking at pictures," said Kim. "When you come to my house, I'll show you some of Lee and me."

"And you can see my family photo album too," Hannah exclaimed.

"Let's go right now!" cried Tammy.

It's fun to share the history of your family with relatives and friends.

Even if family members disagree, they still love each other.

Bobby ran all the way home from school. He was excited because his grandpa was coming for dinner. As he opened the front door he heard loud voices.

"Add more charcoal briquettes to the barbecue!" His grandpa sounded angry.

"No. Less charcoal so it heats evenly," said Bobby's dad sternly.

Bobby walked into the backyard. His grandpa called him over. "Come give me a hug."

Bobby shook his head sadly. His dad walked over to him. "What's the matter?"

"Do you hate Grandpa?"

"Of course not. We love each other very much," his father reassured him.

"Then why were you fighting?" asked Bobby.

"We have different ideas about barbecuing. Just because we argued doesn't mean we don't care about one another."

Family members are not always going to agree about everything. Even if they argue, however, it doesn't change the way they feel about each other.

Some families have stepbrothers or stepsisters.

Mitchell was riding his tricycle in front of his house. Jason walked by. "I'm going to the store to get an ice cream cone," he said. "Do you want to come?"

"I can't," replied Mitchell, "my stepbrother Jesse is coming to visit."

"I didn't know you had a stepbrother," said Jason.

"Well, my dad was married before and Jesse is a lot older than me," explained Mitchell. "He's ten."

Mitchell waited in front of his house. He was starting to feel nervous. He usually felt shy around his stepbrother because Jesse was so much older and he only came to visit a couple of times a year.

When Jesse drove up with his father, Mitchell suddenly forgot his shyness. Jesse was very happy to see him and gave him a big hug. The boys' father said, ''Well, I have my two sons together again. This is great. As a special treat, I got tickets to the baseball game tonight.''

You can have a special relationship with a stepbrother or stepsister even if you don't live with them.

Families come in different sizes.

Colette and Kim arrived at Eva's house one day to fingerpaint. Eva took them through the kitchen on the way to the basement. Colette noticed that several people were making lunch. Colette asked, "Do you have visitors?"

"No," said Eva, laughing. "Grandmother, Aunt and Uncle live with us. We have a big house and Mom and Dad like to have lots of our relatives around."

"Doesn't it feel crowded sometimes?" asked Kim.

"Oh no," answered Eva. "I love being part of a big family."

Some families are made up of parents and their children. Other families include aunts, uncles, cousins and grandparents who all live together.

Some families have adopted children.

Hannah, Janice and Tammy were playing in Janice's backyard with their dolls. "My doll is adopted," said Tammy.

"What does adopted mean?" asked Hannah.

"I know," answered Janice. "My dad was adopted by my grandparents. Some people take a child someone else can't look after. They care for it just like it was their own."

"So if I couldn't care for my doll properly, I could let you adopt her?" asked Hannah.

"Yes, that's right," replied Tammy. "And I could adopt your doll if I had space for her and enough money to look after her and I promised to love and care for her."

Some children are adopted by a family and are loved and cared for by that family.

Family occasions are special times.

Finally it was parents' night at the school. Dylan went with his father, and Janice and Jason went with both of their parents. Eva arrived with her entire large family.

The school gym was covered with the children's pictures and projects. The teachers served punch and cookies. The children introduced their families to each other and pointed out the things they had made. Everyone had a wonderful time.

There are many different kinds of families. There are some families with one child and one parent. Other families have adopted children or stepchildren. Some large families include aunts, uncles and grandparents all living together. Each family is very special. Here are some ways you can be a better member of your family:
- Be thoughtful if a relative is sick.
- Make everyone feel included.
- Share responsibilities and memories.
- Support one another when things go wrong.

Printed and bound in U.S.A.